Seven Sacred Directions

A Native American Message of Transformation

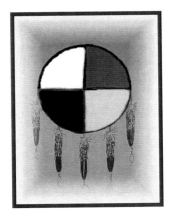

Singing Man

with CheVonne Switzer

Published by
MavenMark Books
A division of HenschelHAUS Publishing, Inc.
2625 S. Greeley Street, Suite 201
Milwaukee, WI 53207
www.HenschelHAUSbooks.com

Please contact the publisher for quantity discounts.
ISBN: 978-159598-156-1

Also available in Kindle format:
ISBN 978159598-180-6

Library of Congress Cataloging Number: 2012940012

Printed in the United States of America.

To Crystal, for always encouraging me to follow my dreams

To my mother Lillian, for never giving up on me when others did

To all the Medicine People of the world

To CheVonne, for her tireless, selfless work
and making this publication possible.

Table of Contents

Preface

What you hold in your hands is the voice of Singing Man. His wisdom and message combine ancient Native American teachings and philosophy with a modern day understanding of personal struggle, transformation, and ultimate awakening.

This work is unending as we seek to provide healing and share the wisdom of Native ways. We are all related. We are all one.

As we walk this earth—our Mother—we ask for and seek acceptance and understanding that there is much a unified People can accomplish and contribute to the greater good.

We understand that this work may not "fix" everyone or be the "correct" or "right" answer for everyone. In sharing this message, we raise our voice and call in an awakening of collaboration and unity—toward the healing of all People.

I am honored to call Singing Man my Grandfather. He is my family. His perspective and wisdom are without definition or quantification. He sacrifices greatly for his family and all those seeking his assistance.

I chose to take part in this work in order to shed light on and bridge the gap between Native and non-Native ways. I invite all to consider the power of inclusion and acceptance as they read this work. This inclusion and acceptance is of ALL People—all our Relations.

Cast aside the preconceptions and prejudice.

Cast aside entitlement and ownership.

Cast aside all that is unknown.

Peel back the layers of time and history. Destroy the mask. Own the here and now.

Know that this work and all who have been a part of it understand and protect all that which is Sacred. We speak and write in a good way to share and provide assistance to all Relations.

We call out to all Relations to join the quest for unified transformation and healing—healing of self, healing of others, and healing of our Mother.

There is much to be gained in unified collaboration and exploration of the space between our perceived differences—illuminating the oneness which is all Relations.

To you and your Relations—*Aho*

=/= CheVonne

EE-NAH-NEE-BAY-EE'S JOURNEY

Many years ago, there was a young man whose name was EE-NAH-NEE-BAY-EE. He wanted more than anything to become a warrior. He belonged to the Rabbit Clan of the Blue Sky People. He was from a well-respected family and was liked by many. All the men of his family were very brave Warriors who had fought in many wars. His great-grandfather, grandfather, father, and uncles on both sides of his family had all been warriors.

The men of his family began to prepare him for war. They told him he would have to travel many miles before he arrived at the battlefield. He began to prepare himself mentally, emotionally, physically, and spiritually for the task. He was trained in the art of warfare for many weeks before getting the approval of the older warriors that he was ready. He traveled to the battlefield, where he met up with several of his fellow warriors, who also began to prepare him for battle. He prayed long and hard that he would not be killed and would live to become a respected warrior for his people.

As he approached the battlefield, thoughts of his family and loved ones ran through his mind. He loved them and missed them all very much. He fought back the tears of his aching heart because that was not the way of a warrior.

When the young man began to fight, he struggled against the urge to run and hide. He was very afraid, but in his heart, he knew it was not the way a warrior should be. He prayed as he began to fight. He began to see visions of spirits and warriors and many things that were sacred to his people. As he continued to fight, he began to slay his enemy. Many of his adversaries lay lifeless in front of him on the battlefield. As much as he hated the bloodshed, he began to enjoy the powerful feeling of being a brave warrior.

Through these battles, he began to be recognized as a warrior who was very brave even in the midst of much chaos. He had been wounded many times, but his most serious wounds could not be seen.

As he traveled back to his encampment and his family, his mind began to see visions of the enemy he had slain. As he tried to sleep through the night, he would be awakened by the smell of blood and the screaming of warriors who were dying on the battlefield.

He tried to adjust to the return into his family and the tribe, but the terrifying visions became stronger and stronger. Spirits would invade his sleep every night and they would awaken him in terror. He was starting to fear for his sanity. Many in his tribe and family thought that he was losing his mind.

He began to use foreign remedies suggested by others to try to purify his mind, body, and spirit, but everything failed. He began using these remedies until his body became so dependent on them that he would crave them when he didn't have them. He began abusing these remedies so much that he became sick and soon lay dying. As he was dying, his mother Killing After came to visit him. She was the only person of his family and tribe who had not given up on him.

As he tried to sleep, he began to witness his own burial in a vision that Creator had given him. In this vision, Creator had let him see all of his family and friends, but none of them could see or hear him because he was a spirit. Sweet Medicine, the youngest of his daughters, came to view his body; she was crying uncontrollably. She was so small that she could barely see onto the death bed where he was lying.

Sweet Medicine said, "Father, why did you leave us? You always taught us to be brave and strong, but look at you. You gave up. You are a coward."

When he could travel, the elders told him of the journey he must make to get rid of the bad spirits who were trying to take over his life. He traveled many miles from the reservation in Oklahoma to the northern reservation of his people in Wyoming. He was very tired after arriving at the Sacred Sundance Grounds of his people.

His Uncle Shakespeare met him when he arrived. Shakespeare was the Keeper of the Sacred Flat Pipe of his People. The old man instructed EE-NAH-NEE-BAY-EE that he must fast in the ceremonial lodge and pray that the bad spirits might leave him. EE-NAH-NEE-BAY-EE agreed and prayed to Red Man, the Sundance Chief of the tribe. The young man subjected and humbled himself to Creator to be released from the bad spirits that were influencing him.

The young warrior sacrificed for four days and nights without food or water and became totally emaciated. He cried to Creator for help. Red Man came to him in the lodge and gave him a special amulet to wear for protection and strength when he prayed to Creator.

The young man asked if this would help him endure his suffering. Red Man replied, "Only if you believe." The young warrior began to dance in the sacred lodge and pray. Creator gave him another vision. He went into a trance-like state and saw many wonderful colors and beautiful things like spirits of family and friends who had gone on to the spirit world. These spirits cheered and encouraged him to be strong and brave.

When he awoke from the trance-like state and came back into consciousness, he was dancing in the sacred lodge again. He looked around at the men who were dancing in the lodge and saw how tired and thirsty they were. They were coughing and choking because their throats were so dry from the dust and heat. He noticed that he was not hungry or thirsty anymore. He felt as if nothing happened to him in his suffering.

Across the lodge, he noticed his ceremonial grandfather, Red Man, looking at him. Red Man nodded to him and walked across the lodge to where the young warrior was standing and said to him, "You will be all right now because you believed."

Before his ceremonial grandfather passed on, he instructed the young warrior that he must help other young warriors who were in similar situations. He instructed him on building and facilitating a smaller version of the main lodge of his people. This lodge is referred to as the "sweat lodge" or "purification lodge." The young man began to assist other warriors who were having difficulty with their lives.

As time passed, the young warrior began to flourish and feel like he was a warrior again. He regained his health and began to walk in beauty again. He was no longer fighting on the battlefield, but rather combating negative spiritual entities all around other young warriors who had been subjected to similar fighting. The young man began to speak and pray for the young warriors who were suffering as he had. He took them into the lodges and helped to purge the negative spiritual entities that were trying to win over their souls.

Some of the young warriors he attempted to help thought they would do it their own way and many of them died. A few, however, were brave enough to ask EE-NAH-NEE-BAY-EE for help because everything they had tried failed. Many of them became valuable members of their families and tribe, and most were able to contribute to the tribe's well-being and sense of community.

That is the story of EE-NAH-NEE-BAY-EE. But it doesn't end there. The translated name of EE-NAH-NEE-BAY-EE is "Singing Man" or "Man Who Sings." It is the name I was given after I came home from fighting in the Republic of South Vietnam in 1971 by the Four Old Men of the Arapaho People, also known as the Blue Sky People. These Four Old Men were all my biological uncles and have since passed on.

I am EE-NAH-NEE-BAY-EE. I was that young warrior. Now, I am an old warrior. The reason I tell this story is because my people learn by storytelling. This is a true story. You are my people, too. I hope you will learn that traditional ways are good and have an honored place in all cultures.

Please consider the "Old Ways" when thinking about the mental health of our people. Therapeutically, these purifications have been helpful for all cultures and beneficial in dealing with Post-Traumatic Stress Disorder (PTSD) from combat, domestic violence, rape, and many kinds of traumatic issues.

I have been free of all mood-altering chemicals since August 8, 1983. Not a day goes by that I don't think of Vietnam. I have made those thoughts my friends now and know that I never have to hurt another living soul as long as I live. War is always the same. Same old stuff, just a different day. If it had not been for the love of my mother, Killing After, and the teachings of my ceremonial elders, I would have died in 1983. The medical staff where I was hospitalized had given me only six months to live.

About this Book

even Sacred Directions is a compilation of stories I have heard for many years. These stories were taught to me by many of my people and the people of other Native American tribes around the United States.

Like many others, I was originally taught that there were Four Directions and learned their meanings. Then, over twenty years ago, one of my elders explained to me that there were really *seven* such directions.

The numbers four and seven are sacred to my people, but I did not understand the full impact of those numbers until I explored the Seven Sacred Directions later in my own life. It is my intention to share these explorations with you in this book.

Let us begin with the number *four*. It is said that the number four is significant to my people because it represents the four directions and the four sentinels or protectors of the linear plane: East, South, West, and North. These directions are depicted on the Medicine Wheel by four different colors and meanings.

The East is associated with the color red, and represents the Morning Star, new beginnings, the season of spring when our Earth Mother is beginning to sprout forth with new life, the newborn, and the MENTAL aspect of the "Two-leggeds," or humans.

The South is represented by yellow, and is associated with the season of summer, when our Earth Mother is at her highest peak of heat and growth, the adolescent, and the PHYSICAL aspect of the Two-leggeds.

The West, represented by black, is also associated with the season of Autumn, when our Earth Mother is starting to get sleepy and preparing to rest, and the adult. This direction is also said to be where the spirits of all that has ever been resides, and represents the SPIRITUAL aspect of the Two-leggeds.

The North and the color white are associated with the season of winter, when our Earth Mother is at rest, the elder, and the EMOTIONAL aspect of the Two-leggeds.

There are also three other directions that are very important. The fifth direction is Mother Earth. She is represented by the color green, the color of foliage when all is at full growth. Mother Earth represents the sacred place from which all life has come. Mother Earth should be as revered as our human mothers, but often is not. We, as the Two-leggeds, have been very disrespectful of our Mother Earth. The elders say that the Two-legged nation comes from Mother Earth and so we are all related through her different shades.

The sixth direction is the plane upon which the Two-legged, Four-legged, Winged, Water creatures, Creepers and Crawlers, reside, and is represented by the color brown.

The final direction is the direction of the Creator. This is the most important of all the directions and is represented by the color sky blue. Often people take this direction for granted and do not treat it with priority. Members of the Two-legged nation often do not beseech this direction until the situation is very bleak. In the military, we used to call such seeking "fox-hole prayers," praying only when things were bad or our lives were in danger. The Arapaho Nation is also referred to as the "Blue Sky People."

All these directions and aspects represent the Medicine Wheel and will be explored fully throughout this book. It is not my intention to exploit anything about the spirituality of the Blue Sky People or any culture. My intention, instead, is to share these stories for the good of all people of Mother Earth, as we say in our Indian communities, "in a good way." If these Seven Sacred Directions are followed, they will change your life and change your perception of the way all life should be.

My people have passed down many of the things I tell for generations. They are not secrets. Some of the things have also been written about by other cultures around the world. Some of the stories I tell are of my own experiences. Many are stories that have been told to me. In any case, this book is one of faith, love, and hope for all of Creator's children.

The Two-leggeds, or humans, should balance and harmonize with each other and Mother Earth. She is being exploited, raped, burned, and all of her resources used until one day, she will have nothing to give anymore. We need to realize that unless we act and act fast, many drastic and untimely changes will continue to occur.

These Seven Sacred Directions truly offer a way to live your life with love, respect, and dignity. I suggest that *Seven Sacred Directions* be read for seven days, one chapter a day. This will give you time to reflect on yourself and all your relations.

The working sections of this book will allow you to put your feelings and thoughts into perspective and help you reflect on what is really important to you. You will possibly find yourself pulling away from Western thinking and immersing yourself into traditional Native thinking.

You might say, "But I'm not native." You don't have to be. Many of you are Native at heart. Some of you I know personally; others I have yet to meet. Regardless, Western thinking, also deemed "left-brain thinking," is more logical, sequential, rational, analytical, objective, and looks at parts. Native, or "right-brain thinking," is more random, intuitive, holistic, synthesizing, subjective, and looks at wholes. Right brain thinking is more abstract and allows us to become more accepting of people, places, and things. Maybe we should use this circle to connect us all in a way that we are all one.

East ~ Red ~ Mental

The East direction is represented by the color red, where the sun rises and everything is fresh and new. It is also represented by the season of spring, where everything is just beginning to bloom. This direction is also symbolic of the infant.

East is also associated with the MENTAL component of your Medicine Wheel. Your Medicine Wheel is made up of seven distinct parts or directions that make you who you are. If these parts are not in balance, your life will probably not function properly.

Man's actions are a direct result of his thinking. People manufacture their own physical and mental agony by unbalanced decisions and actions regarding personal, business, or social relations. Our brains are electric storehouses for memories recorded upon them as a result of the experiences of our senses. The brain is the nerve center of all parts of the body, which motivates the body to perform various functions. The brain of a person is not the mind.

Very few people think at all. Sound strange? Very few people think about anything at all. They simply respond to their senses and do very little original planning, assembling, designing, or creating. Many people simply imitate the thinking and behaviors of others and act automatically. The herding instinct is very strong in humans. In their need to belong to a group and the fear of being alone, people imitate the behaviors of the majority without thinking of their actions and the impact on themselves or others.

The brain stores, organizes, retrieves, and analyzes bits and pieces of information. Western culture tends to be "left-brained thinking," using mind/brain-centered functions as the means to solve problems, collect and analyze information, and make decisions based on the analysis. The mind/brain used in this manner is an incomplete tool. It does not include the intuition or deep intention contained in every person. It does not include that moment of knowing, when the light bulb goes off, that moment of inspiration, directly from Creator. How often do we ask ourselves *what does my heart say*? Our heart often says something completely different from our mind/brain conclusion.

The East is associated with the CIRCLE. In many cultures, people believe "what goes around, comes around" or "you reap what you sow." In some cultures, it is called the Universal Law of Karma. For every action, there is a reaction. This is conscious choice-making. We live in a world of choices. Some of these choices are conscious and some are unconscious. Because many of our choices are unconscious, we don't perceive them to be choices. This is false. Everything happening to you in this moment and in past moments is the direct result of active choices you have made.

Most of our choices are the direct result of conditioning to people, places, and things. What happens to a dog if you kick it every time you pass by? After walking by it many times, you continue to kick it and then the last time, you just walk by and the dog still jumps. It has been conditioned to the stimuli you have provided.

As a Vietnam veteran, I have worked with many combat veterans and have noticed that many of us who fought in a war are conditioned by the stimuli we received while in combat. We are conditioned to the world around us. Many combat veterans are hyper-vigilant. When we walk into an area that is unknown to us, we begin to scan our surroundings for anything that appears to be out of place. If we are in a wooded area, we scan for any kind of movement. That is the way we have been conditioned. When we hear loud noises, we react to them, sometimes in ways we don't like. We are so conditioned to react that we respond unconsciously.

Many of us—civilians and veterans alike—even though we have the choice, are the direct result of conditioned reflexes that are triggered by people, places, and things into predictable outcomes of behavior. If we begin to make choices of the unconscious to the conscious, we will have empowered ourselves into conscious choice making. This mere act is very empowering.

Most of us know right from wrong. If this is so, then why do we consciously make wrong choices? Often we do not weigh the consequences of our choices. Of all the choices we make, there is always one that is the right choice.

If you make the right choice in a situation, your choice will support you and all those who are concerned with that choice. If you make the wrong choice, you most certainly will know in your heart, the feelings of discomfort that choice has given you. You will also begin to see the effects of that choice on others.

Because your heart is the center of your feelings toward your choices, it will either show you comfort or discomfort. If you pay close attention to your body when you make a choice, it will let you know. If you make a choice and there is comfort involved, then it might be the right choice. If your body sends a message of discomfort, it might be the wrong choice.

In August 1983, I witnessed how greatly the decision to stop using mind-altering chemicals would influence my own life and the lives of those around me. I had lost all hope for my life and was drinking myself to death. I was admitted into the Clinton Regional Hospital in Clinton, Oklahoma. I had been hospitalized there because I was literally hemorrhaging from every opening of my body. The doctor used an exploratory camera to assess the damage that my chemical addiction had brought on. He simply stated, "Singing Man, if you don't stop drinking, you will be dead in six months."

East ~ Red ~ Mental

At the time, I didn't care if I lived or died. Life appeared meaningless to me. I had spent many months in Vietnam and had been exposed to many dangers. Why should I care if I lived?

I did, however, make the decision to stop drinking that day because while I was sedated, Creator allowed me to see a vision of my own funeral. The thought of dying didn't frighten me, but what did not sit well was the thought that my children would to have to witness their father dying drunk. In my vision, my youngest daughter at the time called me a coward as she viewed my lifeless body. Nobody had ever referred to me as a coward. After all, I belonged to four warrior societies. How could I be a coward?

She was right, though. In my attempts to be what I thought was a man, I did nothing but disrespect the life Creator had blessed me with by running from life and my responsibilities. I thought a man was supposed to be a person who took what he wanted, drank hard, lived hard, and slept with as many females as came along. Unfortunately, there are many men out there who still feel and live this way.

Today, my thoughts of what a warrior should be are much different from those I once had. I now believe a warrior is one who protects his family, community, and country, and also takes time to talk to his relations, as well as listen. When I speak of relations, I am speaking of everything with which we are in relationship in the Universe. That is all things. A warrior should be kind, compassionate, loving, and nurturing, and one who respects all women. In our belief system, women are the "life-givers" and are also very sacred in our spiritual beliefs and ceremonies.

There was a feeling of rightness about my decision to stop taking the mood-altering chemicals, but at the time, I wasn't quite aware of the impact. As the cobwebs cleared and sanity began to come back to me, I could feel in my heart that I made the right decision. That was August of 1983 and I have yet to regret my decision on that hot summer day.

The more you become consciously aware of the choices you make in your life, the more spontaneously correct your choices will be. We all have made negative decisions that have influenced, and may continue to influence, aspects of our lives today. Because of poor choices, we might choose to correct them.

One way to correct these decisions is to sacrifice for those things you might consider to be negative choices, resulting in negative consequences. Because of the constant give and take of the Universe, these choices may come back to you, as in the circle. A belief of my Native people is to sacrifice for those decisions you might have made in error. Fasting, as well as participating in rituals and in ceremony, are ways to sacrifice. We often use different kinds of ceremony to rid ourselves of impurities we may have picked up unsuspectingly. These are often done in a strict ritualistic way.

We may then fast for a period of time and ask Creator to forgive us for past transgressions we might have committed. We may also ask Creator for a vision or vow to dance in one of our sacred lodges. In doing so, we believe that

Creator will forgive us if our intentions and hearts are good. This also has another advantage. It is believed that sacrificing in this way will benefit not only us, but also our families and other relations. In other words, we sacrifice for the people.

Another way to respect these past negative events is to learn from them. If there is something that happens to you in a negative way, ask yourself, "How can I learn from this? or What is the lesson in this situation?"

If a person loses a limb, that person can either make the decision to feel sorry for himself or learn to live with the disability. My brother Robert was born without femur bones in his legs. He could have pitied himself and been bitter about his situation, but he was not. He now lives in Oklahoma with his wife, drives a vehicle, and works in the security division of one of our tribal casinos. He made the choice many years ago to work with what Creator gave him and do the best he could. I have much respect for my brother.

A few years ago, I worked with at-risk adolescents from a shelter in Michigan. Two boys at the shelter made the decision to go AWOL from the center. They fashioned blankets to disguise themselves in their beds. They made their escape in the early morning. They chose to steal a car and make a getaway to a larger town north of the center. They also chose to use chemicals that probably helped them make other irrational decisions on that fateful early morning.

Not thinking of the consequences of their actions and probably impaired while driving, they drove along at a high rate of speed and failed to make a curve in the road. They hit a tree and the boy who was the passenger in the car died instantly. The other boy, who was driving, survived only to end up in the Intensive Care Unit in a hospital. After being nursed back to health, he faced numerous charges, including manslaughter for the death of his companion. He has to live with the decision he made that day, as well as the tragic loss of his friend. His life is forever changed.

These are just a few examples of the challenges I have witnessed others facing. Everyone who is human faces challenges, some larger, some smaller. Many remain with us throughout our lifetimes, and sometimes, we hang on to things that have happened in the past.

We can rid ourselves of past negative events through meditation and prayer. We can share the experience with others in a therapeutic setting, talk over the episode with an experienced professional, and forgive ourselves.

Forgiveness plays an intrinsic part of healing from trauma. You can choose to forgive yourself, as well as others, for decisions that have been made. Otherwise, you will relive the negative experiences of your actions over and over again. If you choose to be a conscious choice-maker, you will begin to make the right choices almost without thinking of it. It does take time and practice, but we owe it to ourselves. When conscious choice is practiced daily, serenity, tranquility and peace will come.

Think of the concept of the circle. With the circle, there is strength. We are unified in our efforts. Without the circle, we have nothing. That is why almost everything done by indigenous people takes place in the circle. The Medicine Wheel, ceremonies, pow-wows, our Talking Circles—all include this circular movement. This is how we maintain strength.

This concludes the first direction. I recommend reading about one direction every day, committing time to the chapter-related meditation, and doing the work presented in the sections following each chapter.

Since many of our cultures do well with ritual, the traditions and written exercises of the following seven directions are but suggestions to follow to assist you and to provide structure.

As you think about the first direction, the East, and the tradition of the circle, complete the exercises on the following pages.

The Tradition of the East

The Circle

Today I will put the tradition of the EAST and the circle in my life by taking the following steps:

1. Today I will cleanse myself in ceremony to rid myself of any impurities I may have picked up unknowingly. I will also meditate, once in the morning and once in the evening. I will transcend my past and ask Creator for forgiveness. I will forgive myself. I will accept where I am today. Creator, grant me the serenity to accept the things I cannot change and the wisdom to know the difference.

2. Today I will consciously be aware of every choice I make in every moment. By witnessing these choices, I will know that every choice I make in the "here and now" will have consequences in the future.

3. By making good choices, I will be aware of the changes in my body, mind, and spirit. I will also be aware of the consequences of the choices I make. I

will ask myself, "Will this choice bring me serenity, tranquility, peace, or despair?" I will also take into account the people who might be affected by the choices I make.

4. I will ask Creator, my heart, and my ancestors for guidance in my choices.

Written Exercises for the
Traditions of the East

Write the answers to the following exercises in this book or on a separate sheet of paper or notebook so you can contemplate your own thoughts and writings for more clarity and meaning.

1. Recall a choice you made without really thinking about it, one that had far-reaching, negative consequences. What were those consequences?

2. Recall a choice you made when you gave it conscious thought before you made the decision, and it had positive results. What were the results?

3. Write an example that you can remember when you wished you had made a different choice.

4. What steps will you take to forgive yourself for this choice?

Notes

South ~ Yellow ~ Physical

The South is represented by the color yellow on the Medicine Wheel. This direction is associated with summer, when all things are at their greatest growth. South is where the warm air comes from. South is also symbolic of the adolescent.

South is associated with the PHYSICAL component of the Medicine Wheel. Our bodies respond to different thoughts and emotions. The chemical processes within are created and depend upon the type of emotion we are feeling. When an individual thinks about pleasure and feels hopeful about life, the body changes into a relaxed state where certain chemicals are released and healing can occur. When an individual is angry, different chemicals are released in the body, creating stress on various organs, especially the liver and pancreas. If the stress continues for extended periods of time, illness may result.

Our physical bodies sometimes do things we do not understand. We crave certain foods or drugs and do not comprehend why we keep using them when we promised ourselves that we would not. We do not understand why we crave that drug or food. The same goes for sex, gambling, or any behavior we crave. We do not understand that craving is triggered by a chemical reaction. We use certain drugs for comfort when we are lonely, depressed, or afraid. Emotions trigger chemical reactions, which then trigger cravings for certain foods, drugs, or behaviors.

Some negative examples of ways some people handle negative emotional situations are through the use of nicotine, caffeine, alcohol, drugs, sex, gambling, and other addictive behaviors. Positive alternatives when dealing with stress or challenging emotions are through prayer, meditation, exercise, faith, love, and hope.

An example of the mystery of the physical and mental aspects of our Medicine Wheel is the relationship between our bodies and our minds. Individuals can actually slow or accelerate their heartbeats through visualization exercises in their minds. If they become frightened, the heartbeat accelerates. If they meditate, their heartbeat slows down. Some automatic body functions can be adjusted by the mind.

Have you ever heard a beautiful song that moved you to tears or witnessed an awe-inspiring sunset that left you breathless? Or looked at a newborn child with such love and affection that you were speechless? All of these things moved you. They pulled at your heartstrings and made you feel connected to your emotions.

Physically, they connect you to the circle of what is, and to what is important to you or those around you. This physical connection can also help in your healing process of yourself or the healing process of those who are important to you. I have been witness to several healings where the ill person was instructed to pray with the healer. The patients were also instructed that unless they believed what is about to happen, no amount of prayer or healing could help them. It comes again from the circle, where everything is connected to everything else.

When the emotional, mental, spiritual, and physical parts of the Medicine Wheel combine with each other, anything is possible.

I have witnessed things that I cannot fully explain by Western standards. I only know *that* I experienced what I experienced. I have seen people recover from terminal illnesses, including heart problems, when the prognosis was thought to be hopeless. I have seen full recovery of other ailments in many. This not only happens in my culture, but in many cultures that truly believe in the power of healing through Creator.

How do you explain miracles? Can you only explain what you can see?

How do you explain a person's recovery from what appeared to be beyond Western medicine's ability to heal? We live in a culture where we have to analyze all things. Sometimes things just cannot be analyzed. Some can only believe what the eyes can see, not from what they cannot.

Physically, how do we account for a small-framed woman lifting a very heavy object off of her badly injured child when it is normally physically impossible for her to do so? How about athletes pushing themselves to the brink of collapse and then winning the contests in which they were competing?

I remember an event while in basic training in the U.S. Army in May 1970 at Fort Lewis, Washington. We had been on a "forced march" of twenty miles with full backpacks and all weapons, or approximately forty to fifty pounds of extra equipment we had to carry throughout the ordeal. The night we were completing our march, several of the soldiers literally fell to the wayside, where an ambulance picked them up. I remember wanting to quit, wanting to give up, but I kept hearing my dad's voice in my head saying, "Don't you give up! Don't you quit!" Physically, I was in such pain I just wanted to cry, but instead, I started to pray, "Please God, help me. Give me strength. Give me courage. Don't let me quit."

Then the drill sergeant yelled at the top of his lungs, "OK, Alpha Platoon, let's show these ladies how tough you are." The sergeant yelled again, "Alpha Platoon, double time." Hearing those words, I wanted to cry out in agony but instead, held my head high and said, "Stay with me, Lord." We ran all the way into our company area before any of the other platoons could get there. I remember feeling a surge of adrenaline pumping through my exhausted body.

Pushing me, forcing me to run and run and run. I couldn't believe it when we reached our barracks. We had done the impossible. We had not quit. We kept pushing ourselves after we connected with the other components of our Medicine Wheels.

After it was over, I asked several of my buddies how they had dealt with the pain and exhaustion. Most of them replied, "I prayed to God or Jesus to get me through the pain." It was true; we all wanted something so much that we went into a "zone," a place where there was no pain.

Such a "zone" is a place we have all been at one time or another, a place of refuge and of hope, where anything is possible if we believe and have faith. It is a place of sacredness where we have the choice to ask Creator for relief. So it is with our lives. If we get to the point of exhaustion and hopelessness, it is our choice to ask for relief. When we do, Creator will relieve us from the earthly pain.

The South is also associated with the GIVEAWAY. Native People have a tradition in their respective tribes. The tradition differs from tribe to tribe, but the basic idea is usually the same. When we choose to honor someone for something, we give that person something of value to us. We believe that when we give something away, it will come back to us in return.

It is still common practice among my people to have giveaways. These are usually held during major powwows, funerals, or dances. I have been witness to several of these ceremonies, where items like money, blankets, material goods, weapons, and so on, have been given to honor the receiver. I have even seen horses given away. During the Oklahoma oil boom of the 1970s, I saw brand-new automobiles given to people being honored. It is not uncommon for a family to give almost all of its possessions to honor a son or daughter during a give-away. Among my people, we believe that you are rich by what you give to others. Many elders from different cultures have explained to me, "To keep what you have, you have to give it away."

If you interfere with this constant give and take, you are interfering with the very life force of the Universe. To get love, you must give love. To get respect, you must give respect. If you want fidelity in a relationship, you must give fidelity. Give and take goes far beyond intimate relationships, and includes relationships you have with friends, peers, co-workers, or even people you meet for the first time. You must give what you wish to receive. Relationships are always give and take. What goes around comes around.

A few years ago, I wanted to honor several veterans I knew and respected. I gave away several cherished eagle feathers to fellow combat veterans during a Giveaway. One of my family members noticed that I only had a few feathers left in my collection. She told me not to give away any more or I would be left with nothing. I ignored her because I remembered what the elders told me of the circle: when you treat people well, it will come back to you many fold. I only had four eagle feathers remaining when I received a whole eagle carcass in another giveaway.

Many things can increase by giving them away. For instance, money is a flow of energy. You must not let money stagnate. It must keep moving. To receive wealth, you must give it away. Anything of value in your life only multiplies when it is given away.

However, please be aware that if you give something grudgingly or expect something in return, there is a great loss of energy in the giving.

Happiness is also another important factor in the giving and receiving. The intent of giving and receiving is to bring happiness for the giver, as well as the receiver. It will surely come back to you many times over.

When you give from the heart, unconditionally, it is a true gift. When you feel joy in the act of giving, this energy increases many times over. To get what you want, help others get what they want.

People might say, "I have nothing to give." The truth is, everyone has have something to give. You can give a simple smile or a thank you, a note of appreciation, a hug, a compliment, or a prayer. Why not try a simple test for the next thirty days. Run off business cards or simply write on pieces of paper. "This card is redeemable for one hug. Keep this card and pass on to another person." Do this for one month and see how positive it makes you feel, as well as those who receive it.

Prayer also has much power to affect those around you. I have seen the power of prayer. A simple saying comes to mind, "If you pray, don't worry. If you worry, don't pray." These simple conscious thoughts of prayer have the power to change the world.

Remember, the most important gifts to people are not material things. Give the gift of attention by listening to others. Give affection. People want to know they are appreciated. Tell your significant other how much he or she means to you. Send a note. Give a hug. These things do not cost a thing except time. Surely we all have the time. Silently give a prayer when you meet someone. Even if the person is rude, he or she especially needs prayer. When you visit someone's house, take a gift or give a simple flower.

Do this for the next few days and your life will change forever. You will be amazed at what you get in return. When you give of yourself without the thought of getting anything in return, the energy of spirit in the Universe and Creator will fill you with amazing joy and happiness.

I have heard many Native peoples say that what knowledge we have, we must keep. We shouldn't share our knowledge with non-Natives. I agree that we have had many things taken from us and even as I write these words, there are those who will abuse this knowledge for themselves and for material gain. I have to remember what my first ceremonial grandfather told me in 1984 during our ceremonies. He said, "There are people who will try to take these things from us and use them for profit. Don't be concerned, Grandson. Creator has a way of taking care of those who abuse these sacred things. They will only hurt themselves or those they love if they do these things. It's all right to pray with others as long as you don't let them know everything of our medicine."

For that reason, I pray with many people from all walks of life. There is ritual to the way we do things. I will not ever disrespect my People by abusing my medicine. To keep what I have, I must also share it with others. As I have said, these ways come from people around the world and what I write here is common knowledge.

This concludes the second direction, the South. As you complete your reading, I again suggest that you take time to consider what you have read and how practicing the traditions of this direction will assist you.

The Tradition of the South

The Giveaway

Today, I will put the tradition of the SOUTH and the Giveaway in my life by taking the following steps:

1. Today, I will cleanse myself in ceremony to rid myself of any impurities I may have picked up unknowingly. I will also meditate, once in the morning and once in the evening. I will ask my ancestors for guidance in my journey. I will transcend my past and ask Creator for forgiveness. I will forgive myself. I will accept where I am today. I will change those things I can and ask Creator for wisdom to know the difference.

2. In my journey today, for whomever I meet, I will bring a gift. I will give something to everyone with whom I come into contact. It may just be a prayer, a compliment, or a pleasant thought. I will give without expecting anything in return.

3. Today, I am worthy of all the good things Creator has given me. I will be aware of not only the Two-leggeds, but of all Mother Earth's creatures. I will receive the gifts of light, air, sun, and the Universe. I will accept gifts of others in whatever forms they may come.

4. Today, I will circulate serenity, tranquility, peace, and love to all those I come in contact with. I will silently pray for their joy, laughter and happiness.

Written Exercises for the

Tradition of the South

Write out your responses to the following exercises in this book or on a separate sheet of paper or notebook so you can contemplate your own thoughts and writings for more clarity and meaning.

1. Recall a time when you gave something to someone without expecting anything in return. How did it make you feel?

2. Recall a time when you received something from someone when you did not expect anything. How did it make you feel?

3. Explain what it means to you to give and receive.

4. The traditions of the South suggest that we should give without concern for what we feel we should receive in exchange. Are you truly giving and receiving in the traditions of the South? If not, how might you consider changing your behavior to strengthen the habit of giving and receiving?

West ~ Black ~ Spiritual

On the Medicine Wheel, the West direction is represented by the color black. West is the direction in which the spirit world lies and all that has ever been dwells as spirit. It is also associated with the season of autumn, when everything is starting to get sleepy and ready to rest. This direction is symbolic of the adult.

West is also associated with the SPIRITUAL component of your Medicine Wheel. When you understand this reference point of your own spirit, you begin to understand your pure potential. The opposite of spirit reference is object reference. Object reference is influenced by objects outside of Spirit, which include people, places, and things. When we seek the approval of others, our thinking and behavior is always in anticipation of what others will think. This is fear-based thinking.

Some time ago, I was employed at one of the Oklahoma state prisons as the Substance Abuse Coordinator for the inmates. I dealt with all kinds of criminals who were behind bars. One case in particular has stuck in my mind over the years—a young man who was a career criminal. His was a classic case of object reference. He appeared to come from a good home and family. After much counseling with him, I found out his family members were devout Christians. They had tried their best to raise him in a positive environment within the confines of their low-income background.

The young man did not like being poor and began to get in trouble with the law, stealing and associating with the wrong kinds of friends who pursued a lifestyle of money, jewelry, and women. He was very attracted to that fast-paced lifestyle. He was following a lifestyle of fear-based power, or the illusion of power was a false power. Instead of his real power being spirit-based, it was fear-based.

His new way of life broke his mother's heart. I spoke to her on several occasions; she just wanted her son to "find God" and lead a good life.

After being released from incarceration, the young man became homeless, tried to rob a convenience store in Oklahoma City, Oklahoma, and was shot and killed by the store owner. I attended his funeral and grieved with his family. This is an extreme example of object reference; in most cases, it is not so severe.

When living with object reference, we have the overwhelming need for power and control. This fear-based mechanism is born of our need to control situations. Fear-based power is not real power. The pure power of spirit emerges when we do not need to control, when we do not need the approval of others, and we do not live in the presence of fear.

Your ego is your self-image; it is the role you play or your mask. This mask needs to have the approval of others. If you live in fear, the mask's power is sustained. Some people are often afraid to remove the mask because they feel it is all they have.

A personal example of this happened in the early 1980s, when I was first becoming a counselor in the field of addictions. Many of my clients and patients were street-smart criminals, people who were used to intimidating anyone they came into contact with. I was intimidated as well, to say the least. All of the education and training I had received to deal with addicts and alcoholics went out the window. At times, I was literally in fear for my own safety.

I felt I had to wear the mask of a Vietnam veteran who was not afraid of anything. I became as intimidating as some of my clients. I thought that in order to deal with the hard-core clientele, I must become one of them in order to gain their respect. There is only one huge problem when trying to be therapeutic with such a mind-set: in my opinion, it doesn't work.

After years of frustration in dealing with such clients, I became quite disenchanted with being a counselor. I felt that I was the one who must change. In other words, the only one I could change was me. I became less and less intimidating and more and more understanding, compassionate, and caring. Then I was finally able to do much better work as a counselor and did not have to try to intimidate anyone. I gave clients the choice of either doing what they were supposed to do and what was expected of them, or behaving negatively. When people have an option of making choices, and truly weigh the outcome, they will usually make the right decision. To my surprise, most of my clients began to change and heal as I did.

Your true spirit does not need masks to sustain it. Your spirit and soul are completely free of those negative things. True spirit is not fearful of any challenge, and feelings are not hurt by criticism. The power of spirit is full of humility and does not feel superior to anyone.

In spirit reference, you are not fearful of any challenge. True power is when you have respect for all people, places, and things, yet do not feel superior to anyone.

Object reference, on the other hand, is fear-based power and thus false power. If people need objects to make them feel better and sustain their self-worth, that is ego-based power or false power, and it only lasts as long as the symbols of money, title, or prestige are maintained. When those symbols are gone, so is the power.

The power of spirit reference is permanent because it is based on the knowledge of spirit. This power seems to draw people to you. It also draws things to you that you want. This power comes from being in a state of humility. When you are in this state, you are close to your spirit, but also the spirit of all things.

You can start to realize your full potential by doing certain things. Daily meditation, relaxation, and seeking silence are positive actions. Becoming non-judgmental and spending time with Creator and Mother Earth will help to cultivate the wonderful attributes of bliss, creativity, and freedom.

Begin this process by setting a little time aside each day to be in silence. Get away from distractions that drain your energy, like television, radio, cell phone, or whatever it is you have become dependent upon. If you live in a place where there is constant noise, use earplugs and an eye mask when meditating to prevent the noise and light from coming in. I like to put on a beautiful CD of Native flute melodies, lie flat on the floor, and go into total relaxation. I suggest that people meditate and relax for no less than one-half hour twice per day. As you become more accustomed to this regimen, longer periods are not uncommon.

When you continue with this experience, your internal dialog will begin to still. Soon, you will be in a state of complete relaxation or alpha state. This is because you, as the spirit or self, are the decision-maker. It takes a little time to become accustomed to this alpha state, but after a while, you begin to reach this plane or state of consciousness without much trouble.

Once you achieve the alpha state of relaxation, you will begin to realize your maximum potential. If you do such relaxation exercises for thirty minutes in the morning and thirty minutes in the evening, you will begin to start realizing bliss, creativity, and infinite organizing power.

In this state of calm, you can begin to introduce any intention you may wish. You might be struggling with a relationship, education, or clarity. When you introduce your intent, it will go out like a ripple on a pond. It will keep expanding and resonating and become a part of your spirit. It will all be a part of you and will become stronger. If you are sincere, it will be realized.

A personal story might illuminate what I mean. After years of struggle with chemical additions, and trying many things that didn't work, in August 1983, a therapist who was working with me asked if I had ever tried affirmations. At that time, I didn't even know what affirmations were. He went on to explain that these are statements or intentions that you write on a piece of paper and then say as many times a day as possible. Then he asked me what I wanted most out of life. I was puzzled, since I could not even remember believing I was worthy or good enough to achieve what I wanted.

The therapist then gave me an assignment. "Today, you will start looking at yourself as a worthy human being." He asked me to state my intention, write it down, believe in it, and then say it as many times as I could. He told me to write my intentions, my messages to myself, on sticky notes, and put them where I could see them and speak their words out loud. I started writing:

"Today, I am worthy of all good things Creator has given me."

"I learn from my mistakes and don't make them again."

"I am Creator's child, and Creator does not make mistakes."

"I will not use any mind-altering chemicals today."

"I am more tolerant, loving, and compassionate to people."

"I always put Creator first in my life."

I posted those sticky notes in conspicuous places where I could see them every day. They really helped me for the longest time. To this day, if I find myself struggling with an issue, out come the sticky notes. They did more for me than I ever realized.

Another way of realizing your maximum potential is to practice non-judgment. We constantly evaluate and classify everything as good or bad, right or wrong. We all know at least one person who constantly takes inventory. He or she constantly nags or complains or gossips about how someone else dresses, how overweight someone is, or how many people someone else is sleeping with. When people do these things, they are trying to avert attention from themselves. They usually have many flaws they are trying to disguise by calling attention to others. When people live in such a negative state of mind, they constantly drain the life energy from themselves and others. Their internal dialog is in constant turmoil and full of negative energy. This squeezes the peaceful space between their thoughts.

In that space lies the inner stillness that connects you to your maximum potential or power. When you squeeze that space by being judgmental, you constrict the power of your maximum potential. Being non-judgmental creates peaceful silence in your mind.

You can begin this process an hour at a time by saying, "For the next hour, I will not be judgmental." Then you can expand this intention slowly as you master more and more time. You can also access this tradition of your maximum potential by exercising silence, meditation, relaxation, and non-judgment.

I have a wonderful sister whom everyone affectionately refers to as DJ. To my knowledge, she has never said a negative thing about anyone. Her beautiful spirit is full of love, compassion, and empathy for all people. I have learned so much from her. Even when someone is not very nice to her, she will pray for the other person. It is just her way. People just want to be around her, to soak up the very essence of her spirit. She draws people to her like a magnet.

Another practice is spending time with Mother Earth and all of creation. This will give you insight into the workings of Creation and show you the true meaning of "We are all related." It will offer you instances of how we, as the Two-leggeds, are related to all of Creation, inanimate as well as animate.

During the sacred Purification Lodge when the fourth round ends, the flap is raised on the door of the lodge, participants emerge and shout "We are all related." This lets all of Creation know that we are in complete harmony with all of existence. When you learn to appreciate the air, water, fire, and all of Mother Earth, you will begin to see your maximum potential as a Two-legged.

Your maximum potential is the essence of all material wealth as life energy. Being centered in the true meaning of your spirit, you will have no fear,

3. I will sit silently with Mother Earth and appreciate everything she has given me. I will be witness to all of Creation and realize how, "We are all related." I will appreciate a beautiful smile, a sunset, or a bird singing. I will silently listen to all of Mother Earth as my umbilical to her connects me to all of creation.

4. Today I will practice non-judgment. I will not judge anything that happens today. I will be very careful not to take personal inventory of others. Through this day, I will remind myself not to judge people, places, or things.

Written Exercises for

Traditions of the West

Write out these exercises in this book or on a separate sheet of paper or in a notebook so you can contemplate your own thoughts and writings for more clarity and meaning.

1. What do object reference and spirit reference mean to you? Are you able to spirit reference? How?

2. How does it feel as you are able to meditate, relax, sit in silence, and be non-judgmental? Is it a positive experience for you?

3. In your silent meditation, visualize your intention of doing something positive in your life. What was this intent? Do you feel your intent will come to fruition?

4. How do you feel about spending time with Mother Earth? Can you feel the connection to her and all of Creation as you sit in silence? How does it feel?

North ~ White ~ Emotional

North is represented by the color white and the season of winter, where things begin to turn white from the snowfall. It is also symbolic of the elder.

North is associated with the EMOTIONAL component of the Medicine Wheel. We cannot always choose which feelings we will or will not have. Many times, feelings are automatic and give us feedback about how a particular person or situation is affecting us.

Past emotions we have not dealt with have a direct impact the way we respond or react to situations in our current lives. Emotions that are denied or suppressed stay in our body's tissues, glands, muscles, and organs. They sometimes leave when we "re-feel" them or trust for the first time and release them.

One case I had many years ago illustrates the power of suppressed feelings. A young woman I was working with was diagnosed with severe chemical dependency. After spending many hours counseling her, I noted something very familiar: the thousand-yard stare. This is a blank, flat look shown externally when someone is experiencing a terrible or traumatic experience internally. The young woman exhibited many of the symptoms shown by combat veterans returning from war zones. She shared the nightmares, fits of anger, uncontrollable fears, night sweats, and many other issues related to post-traumatic stress, or PTSD. However, whenever I asked about her past, she would deny any problems, defiantly adamant that her chemical abuse was the cause of her bad marriage.

Along with the Western therapy she was receiving, I suggested the Native American purification lodge as an alternative. Surprisingly, she agreed. Her first lodge allowed a breakthrough in her therapy. Once in the darkness and safety of the lodge, as she held the sacred eagle wing, she emerged from her emotional shell. Her hiding was over. She shared with the lodge that as a little girl, she had been molested by her father, and as she got older, her father's advances continued. She had tried to tell her mother, but to no avail. The young woman could not and would not tell anyone of her trauma because of the deep-seated pain.

The PTSD spilled over into all areas of her life and the lives of those around her. She was not capable of having a genuine, intimate relationship with anyone because of the trauma. In fact, her entire family experienced symptoms of PTSD. The young woman also lost jobs because of truancy and being too sick to work, and therefore was not able to provide for her family when she got married and had children of her own.

The young lady completed her chemical dependency treatment and I referred her to an after-care program to address the PTSD. Fast-forward to 2004. ten or fifteen years later. We encountered one another at a function in Oklahoma, where she came up to me, kissed and hugged me. I was startled, to say the least. I did not recognize my former patient at first, so much had she changed. She shared with me that her whole life had changed after the purification lodge. She had been chemical free since that day, had addressed the issues in her life, had remarried, forgiven those who had hurt her, and started living her life as Creator would have it. The encounter so moved me that I cried tears of joy on her shoulder. It is truly amazing what people are capable of when they can work through the trauma and discover the will to live.

There are two basic underlying emotions in all human beings: love and fear. Desire, joy, pleasure, contentment, acceptance, hope, peacefulness, self-esteem, assertiveness, and generosity are a few examples of love-based feelings. Sorrow, apathy, bitterness, jealousy, irritability, depression, rejection, pity, grief, aggression, powerlessness, passiveness, loneliness, and irritability are examples of fear-based emotions. Our bodies produce different chemicals when we feel these two different groups of emotions.

Many of us are afraid of our feelings and emotions. We are afraid that if we allow ourselves to feel, we will lose control. We often deny our feelings, pretend they do not exist, or suppress them. We think that by pretending they are not there, they will go away.

Unfortunately when we suppress our feelings or emotions, they usually surface, often in inappropriate ways.

When I returned from Vietnam after my tour of duty in 1971, I tried to function with some sense of normalcy. I had been subjected to war in a place thousands of miles from my home in Oklahoma and had witnessed many horrible and terrible things while there. Many of the memories were of the men I served with and the atrocities I witnessed. When those thoughts returned to me, it was often in dreams or flashbacks when I was sleeping, or using chemicals to medicate myself. The harder I tried to suppress the thoughts and feelings, the more they intensified until I literally thought I was going mad.

In the heat of battle, to protect itself, your mind itself distances itself from the act you are witnessing. This distance acts as protection for the mind. As a soldier and warrior, I was uncomfortable with the feelings I had when I saw a comrade get killed or wounded. I felt like crying and screaming at the top of my lungs, but that was not the way of a warrior.

To survive, I began to look at life as if it had lost all the sacredness it possessed. I began to look at the lifeless bodies as if they were mere rocks or sticks or anything inanimate so I would not have to associate them as sacred places that had housed the souls of their owners.

When I returned to the United States, I was diagnosed with severe Post-Traumatic Stress Disorder (PTSD) and substance abuse, which sometimes enhance each other. It took me many years before I could come to grips with what I had witnessed in Vietnam. It took me many more before I could start to recover from the trauma.

While often not spoken of, in today's world, fear or fear-based emotions are not acceptable. Some people feel that emotions should not be exhibited at any time. Vulnerability is often perceived as a sign of weakness. It is often important in our society to hide weakness and vulnerability. These attitudes and the motivation to hide weakness and vulnerability are a recipe for illness. It is my belief that if emotions are suppressed, it can be a prelude to depression, substance abuse, PTSD, and even death.

The North direction is also symbolic of the Three Laws of No Resistance. The first law of no resistance is *Acceptance*. If you struggle against a moment or situation, you are struggling against nature and the entire life force of the Universe. When you accept people, places, and things in this very moment, you are experiencing unconditional love for all of creation. You are accepting things as they are in this moment, not as you wish they could be.

The Serenity Prayer, attributed to theologian Reinhold Niebuhr and later adopted by recovery communities, comes to mind:

God grant me the serenity to accept the things I cannot change, the courage to change the things I can, and the wisdom to know the difference.

When you react in frustration to a person, place, thing, or situation, you are reacting to your feelings about that particular thing. Another person cannot make us mad; we make ourselves mad because we react in certain ways to that person.

As a counselor, I have heard many scenarios about life situations and how people react to them. I was once counseling a woman who was experiencing substance abuse problems. She told me how she was the victim of society. She went on and on about how bad her life was and blamed everyone else for her problems. She told of her last arrest and how she had been charged with domestic violence against her sister while in a drunken rage. She blamed her sister for her own inappropriate behavior.

When I worked in the prison system, inmates were notorious for blaming their particular situations on someone else or society. I once overheard an inmate complaining that his situation was caused by our government and that was why he became a criminal. It is always easier to blame others than to accept our situations.

Of course, most people do not experience problems of this magnitude, but how many times have we been in situations when we allowed ourselves to get upset? We did not understand the situation as it was. It was our choice to get upset. No one made us upset.

What about those of us who cannot accept divorce, a traffic fine, a lost job, or worse, the death of a loved one. My grandmother would always set an extra place at the table for her son, who had been killed in a traffic accident while drinking. She could not accept his death and waited for him to return to her home.

Consider asking yourself this question: *How much energy have I wasted today because of non-acceptance of people, places, and things?*

The Second Law of No Resistance is *Taking Responsibility*. Simply stated, this means not blaming anyone, anything, or yourself for your situation in the very moment. Taking responsibility for a situation also means having the wisdom to change the things you can. All problems have solutions. This awareness gives you the opportunity to make adjustments in your life for something much better. As you begin to realize this, every upsetting person, place, or thing will become your teacher.

When uncomfortable situations arise, consider thinking, "This is the way Creator would have this moment so I can learn from it."

In the past, I used to get really upset when relationships went wrong or I couldn't control them. Now I realize Creator gave me those opportunities to learn from. They were in Creator's plan for me. Once I could accept these things, my resistance was minimal, and I took responsibility for my responses to those situations. I was the only one I could control.

Taking responsibility also means that I will try not to make those same mistakes again. I hold no blame for relationships gone badly. Things are as they should be.

A wise person once told me when I was distraught over the breakup of a personal relationship, "You were probably not meant to be with that person so it was good that you broke up with her." At the time it didn't make me feel much better, but now I am so grateful I am not with that person anymore. It was Creator's will.

The Third Law of No Resistance is *Defenselessness*. This means that there is no longer the need to convince or persuade others of your point of view. There is no longer a need to defend yourself. When defending a point of view, a tremendous amount of energy is wasted. Your life will experience resistance when you blame others, become defensive, or not accept things as they are. This resistance increases the more you try to force your point of view. You will prevent an argument if you have no point to defend. You will also experience the "here and now" if you desist from confrontation. The more you resist, the more you can become engulfed in the quicksand of life. It is not that you should become passive, but instead, listen to your heart and your intuition.

One of my favorite quotes is, "The past is history, the future a mystery, and this moment is a gift. That's why they call it the present."

Those words also bring to mind another piece of wisdom I once heard when feeling sorry for myself, "Today is God's gift to you. What you do with it is your gift to God".

When you make an active commitment to accept things as they are, you experience the overwhelming aura of love at its purest level. You experience serenity, tranquility, and peace beyond belief. Take the time to embrace the present. It is a wonderful gift. This gift will be the absence of fear and anxiety and your spirit will be calm. There is no friction or effort down the path of no resistance. It is as it should be. Your life will unfold spontaneously and effortlessly. On this path, your desires will blossom into reality. Practicing the law of no resistance, with its three components—acceptance, responsibility, and defenselessness—will bring you serenity, tranquility, and peace.

An example of how this works is in the Purification Lodge or Sweat Lodge. In the lodge, it is hot, steamy, and sometimes very uncomfortable. I used to fight the situation when I first experienced the lodge. I focused on different reasons why I should not be in there. I could not accept the lodge because of the heat, the sweat, and being uncomfortable. I concentrated on my discomfort instead of concentrating on why I was really in there.

When I began to accept the Lodge as a church or a temple, and started focusing on my prayers, the discomfort left me and I was filled with the over-whelming presence of Creator. This sacred power took care of my discomfort. I no longer felt the heat or was aware of my perspiration or discomfort. I accepted the lodge as a holy sanctuary.

I have been in many lodges since then and accept the experience as a holy union with Creator. When you travel the journey of ACCEPTANCE, RESPON-SIBILITY, and DEFENSELESSNESS, you are on the true path of no resistance and become one with life's pure and holy energy force.

This concludes our reading for today on the traditions of the North. As you complete your reading, I suggest that you take a moment to review and respond to the following pages.

The Tradition of the North
The Path of No Resistance

Today, I will put the tradition of the NORTH and the path of no resistance in my life by taking the following steps:

1. Today, I will cleanse myself in ceremony to rid myself of any impurities I may have picked up unknowingly. I will also meditate, once in the morning, and once in the evening. I will ask my ancestors for guidance in my journey. I will transcend my past and ask Creator for forgiveness. I will forgive myself. I will accept where I am today. I will change those things I can. I will ask Creator for the wisdom to know the difference.

2. Today, I will practice *Acceptance*. I will accept people, places, and things as they are. I will not struggle against nature and the Universe by struggling against this moment. I accept things at this moment, not as I wished they would be.

3. Today, I will take *Responsibility* by accepting things as they are and for those things I see as problems. I will not blame anyone, anything, or myself for the situations as they are at this moment. I will take this opportunity to change the things I can.

4. Today, I will practice *Defenselessness*. I will give up the need to persuade others of my points of view. I will be open to other's points of view. I am not the center of the Universe.

Written Exercises for

Traditions of the North

Write down the responses to these exercises in this book, on a separate sheet of paper, or in your journal so you can contemplate your own thoughts and writings for more clarity and meaning.

1. Can you remember a time when you were so rigid in your point of view that you could not accept anything else? If so, give an example.

2. What does acceptance mean to you? Can you accept yourself and others in this very moment in time? If so, why? If not, why not?

3. What does responsibility mean to you? Are you being responsible in your life at this time? How are you being responsible in your life at this time?

4. Do you still feel the need to defend your point of view? Do you accept other points of view? If not, why not?

Notes

Mother Earth ~ Green
Passion & Purpose

The Mother Earth Direction is represented by the color green. Our Mother Earth is a sacred place where all life springs forth. Since the beginning of time, people of all cultures have developed a reverence for the sacred Mother of all things, maintaining that the Earth is their Mother.

Others have not. There are those who continue to rape, pillage, and destroy the very essence of our Earth Mother.

In traditional Australian Aboriginal society, people learn about their environment first hand and are able to identify the characteristics of animals, plants, sources of food and water, useful materials and even weather conditions. From a young age, Aboriginals are also introduced to the Spirit World through the Dreaming Stories. Each individual's relationship with the land is a very complex spiritual relationship, as he or she is always conscious of the Dreaming ancestors, who Aboriginals believe created all of the geographical features of Mother Earth.

Many cultures around the world have a reverence for our Sacred Mother. Our Sacred Mother is rebelling through earthquakes, weather calamities, and global warming. She will prevail.

Every day, we hear about more and more forests being leveled for greed at the expense of all of us. More and more of our precious air is being polluted, causing a greenhouse effect on our atmosphere and heating up our land. Our rivers, lakes, streams are being contaminated by the refuse of industry, nuclear plants, and mankind. Therefore, there is less drinkable water available for our use.

I recently drove to North Carolina on business and noticed how many forest mountainsides were barren of trees and vegetation. As I travel around the country, I see smog choking our very existence and the future of our children and grandchildren. With the water, it is the same.

Many elders taught the direction of Mother Earth to me. We never forget this direction in our prayers and ceremonies. I tell you this so that we, as Two-leggeds, can start being more respectful to this wonderful Mother and begin to take care of her for all of our relations.

Since the beginning of time, Creator has allowed Mother Earth to provide for our every need. Through vegetation, oxygen is given to us. Through the exhalation of air from our bodies, carbon dioxide is provided back to the plant nation in a sacred symbiotic exchange that is beneficial to both. This energy exchange is the essence of life on our Earth Mother. It is the constant "give and take" of the Universe.

The quality of air we breathe today is greatly compromised, largely because of man. Over the past century, the quality of air we breathe has greatly diminished because of industry and technology. The amount of pollutants released every day by humans is mind-boggling. Nothing frightens us because we continue to use up our oxygen base without seeing any end in sight.

This out-of-balance scenario has resulted in the greenhouse effect on our world today. Our misuse is causing Mother Earth to heat up. Every year, the temperature of our world is continuing to rise. We have caused Mother Earth to run a fever. Will she become sicker and die?

Humans can help her to recover. Have we become so accustomed to our own comfort that we have neglected our Mother? Before it is too late, can we stop global warming? We have to be diligent in our efforts to stop the poisoning of the air we breathe. What is the answer?

Sacrifice is the answer. Our American culture is the most wasteful culture in the world. We need to stop being so ego-centered and start being culture-centered. The typical thinking of humans is self-centered. We have the need to compete, and have more than our neighbors. We have to be better than anyone else. Our comfort is paramount. Our airwaves are bombarded with things to make us feel better. Companies who market their products to us fund our media. When you have a headache, take a pain reliever. Upset stomach? Take an antacid. Are you depressed or anxious? Take an anti-depressant. Worried? Take a drink or chemical to make you feel better.

Our society teaches people that it is good to be pain-free. Does the media ask us to relax, meditate, or pray? No, because that simple way of life doesn't sell products or make money.

I have been a professional counselor for almost thirty years and have incorporated traditional Native American healing practices in Western therapeutic techniques. Specifically, I use the Purification Lodge (sweat lodge) as therapy. When used as a therapeutic tool, the Purification Lodge has been invaluable for treating anger, depression, Post-Traumatic Stress Disorder, and addictions.

Many combat veterans, incest and rape survivors, or people who just want healing, have been treated in the Purification Lodge. Have you seen anything spiritual or holistic like this in the media? Not normally, unless it is on a life/health channel. It just does not sell. We are conditioned that anything worthwhile will cost us monetarily.

The Purification Lodge (or sweat lodge) has been a part of many Native America cultures for centuries. It is a part of who we are spiritually, and the Lodge is sacred to our people.

Out of respect for the sacredness of the Lodge and all those impacted by the events, I will not go into detail, but will say that in 2011, the use of purification lodges made tragic national news. It is my personal understanding that a non-Native claimed he had been trained by Native American ceremonial people and authorized to facilitate lodges. Those who are chosen to facilitate lodges are just that—chosen. Such people are instructed for years before they are allowed to conduct such sacred ceremonies. Lodges built as I was instructed do not allow for overcrowding. If a lodge is run appropriately, there are four rounds and safety is always paramount.

The purpose of a Sacred Purification Lodge is to purify and enhance the participants' connection to the spiritual world. Participation in a lodge should never be considered a feat of strength or physical endurance.

It is my opinion that we should always be careful of the "false prophets" around us. Some of us are so hungry for the answer to life's questions that we become "spiritual butterflies," going from one new thing to another, and never fully landing or trusting our own inner sense of knowing. As I have said in countless workshops and seminars, "The answers you seek are sometimes right in front of you." Natives do not have a monopoly on spirituality. I encourage you to find your spiritual path and trust your spirit guides on this journey.

Valid Native American healers do not charge for what they do in any ceremony. But they do accept offerings as part of the protocol. This is the way they have been instructed by their Medicine People. The reason I tell you this is that there are many Native and non-Natives who call themselves "Shamans" or "Medicine People" and charge for their services. This is not allowable or acceptable by true Native healers. Anyone who is a self-professed Shaman, Healer, or Medicine Person, and requests money or anything of monetary value, should be viewed with a cautious eye.

In many tribes in North America, a person cannot begin to be considered a ceremonial person or healer unless he or she has gone through the many years of ritual and sacrifice required by the Elders. Most certainly, there is no charge for any spiritual blessings.

In most Native ceremonies, Mother Earth is always acknowledged as one of the Sacred Directions. If we do not begin taking care of Mother Earth, she will not take care of us. America is the most wasteful country on Mother Earth. We throw away things that are still usable. We have become a disposable society. Begin sacrificing in respect of our Earth Mother. Begin walking, especially if you live in an urban area. Many places we do business with are within walking distance of our homes or employment. You will do your part to prevent pollution from auto emissions, and become healthy at the same time. Start recycling what you use.

When I was a U.S. soldier in Vietnam, we would throw away empty metal cans. The Vietnamese were very resourceful and would cut out the ends of the cans, cut the remaining pieces down the side, roll the piece of metal out flat, and use the metal squares as shingles or siding for their dwellings.

Sacrifice for Mother Earth. Reduce, reuse, and recycle are words we have heard repeatedly, but do we always follow them? Make it a habit to reduce the things you need or consume. Purchase only things you really need. Eat enough; don't "supersize" everything. Reuse anything that can still be repaired or fixed, or if you no longer wish to have it in your possession, release it to someone else or donate to a charity. Let us each do our share to be a part of the solution and not a part of the problem.

The Mother Earth direction is also associated with the *Tradition of Passion and Purpose.*

At our most basic level, all things in our Universe are comprised of the same recycled elements, hydrogen, oxygen, carbon, nitrogen, and a few other elements in very small amounts. The only difference in these elements from a worm to a flower is the information being fed to them.

Our bodies are not separate from all other things in the Universe, only an extension. We can control our environment and cause things to happen to an certain extent. The teachings of traditional elders are very true. We are all related. What is, was, or shall be is a part of all of us. They meant that we are related to everything in the Universe, animate as well as inanimate. If we develop this thought, we can start to respect all things.

When the traditions of Passion and Purpose are followed, your desire, or Passion, will bring about your goal, or Purpose. If your Passion and Purpose do not violate any sacred laws of the Universe, you can have or be whatever your heart desires. When you begin to introduce your Passion into your Purpose, you activate possibilities beyond your comprehension.

Your focused Passion initiates the universal flow of energy to fulfill your purpose. As long as your Passion remains in the present, it is very effective and could bring your full Purpose into fruition. You can also receive results from very hard work and effort, but the cost is sometimes great. As with all things, work and effort must be in harmony with the rest of your life. If not balanced, illness could result.

An example of Passion and Purpose is the book you hold in your hands. For years, I have wanted to put my thoughts into something that might be able to help people in their lives. My given Native name, *Ee-nah-nee-bay-ee,* means "Man who Sings" or "Singing Man." When my uncles gave me that name in 1971 after I returned from South Vietnam, I was puzzled, to say the least. I questioned them, saying, "But I can't even sing." My Uncle Wes Shakespeare replied, "It's not that you can or cannot sing, but what you will say to people."

They were right, of course. I struggled with fear for years about putting down on paper what I really wanted to say. I always had self-defeating thoughts, like, "I'm not a writer...nobody will want to read what I have to say." However, I kept stating my Passion and intentions to the Universe. As things usually happen, my Purpose began to develop as Creator would have it in His time, not mine.

Sometimes people waste their whole lives thinking about what they have always wanted to do instead of just doing it. I do not want to waste any more time thinking about my Passions and Purpose. Instead, I just pray and let Creator lead me on the path He wants me to take, instead of allowing my fears to sabotage my future. "Let go and let God" is another one of my favorite sayings.

When you follow these steps for fulfilling your Passion and Purpose, your intent will generate its own ultimate power:

1. Meditate and become still. Fill that sacred space in your silence.

2. While in that sacred space, there is nothing but silence. As you begin to encounter thought, express your passion and purpose. If there are many goals, put them on paper. Have your purpose in your mind before you go into the silence. To be successful, go into the silence with that purpose on your mind. Your purpose will be there in your awareness. By simply planting the fertile seeds of your passions, they

will come to fruition when the time is right. You simply release them in your silence.

3. Stay in this state of your spiritual self. Do not let others influence you with criticism or opinions.

4. Do not let your expectations get in the way. Enjoy the journey even if you don't know the outcome.

5. When you release your passion and purpose in this sacred space of silence, they will organize themselves the way they are supposed to be. Creator is in charge of the outcome, not us. Be patient.

My mother, who is a respected elder among the Arapaho Tribe, once told me when I was in turmoil, "You can't change Creator's plan for you. If you live your life in an honorable and respectful way, good things will come to you. Pray for those things you need, not the things you want. If they are meant to be, they will be."

At the time, I did not want to hear this. I wanted a quick fix. I was able to learn from my predicament and the outcome was a good one. Often times, the wisdom of our elders goes unheard by us. I can recall many things that were told to me that I am living today. What goes around, comes around.

As a professional counselor, I have given much advice to others concerning their lives. Some have listened; others have done what they wanted to do. We cannot change people, places, or things. Hopefully, those who didn't listen have learned something from doing it their own way. Some will never learn.

As a simple man involved in ritual and ceremony, I have also spoken to many who did as I suggested. They have gone through many sacrifices and have learned many lessons. Others, who did as they pleased, have had to learn the hard way. Some have even lost their lives because of self-centeredness and being stubborn. Others have come to me later and said, "I wish I would have listened to you at the time because maybe I wouldn't have had to endure all the heartache."

This concludes our reading of the Mother Earth direction. As you complete your reading for today, I suggest you consider the following pages as well.

The Direction of Mother Earth
The Tradition of Passion & Purpose

I will put the direction of Mother Earth and the tradition of Passion and Purpose in my life by taking the following steps:

1. Today, I will cleanse myself in ceremony to rid myself of any impurities I may have picked up unknowingly. I will also meditate, once in the morning and once in the evening. I will ask my ancestors for guidance in my journey. I will transcend my past and ask Creator for forgiveness. I will forgive myself. I will accept where I am today. I will change those things I can. I will ask Creator for wisdom to know the difference.

2. I will make a list of all my passions. I will take a copy wherever I go. Before I meditate and go into the sacred silence, I will focus on my list of passions. When I go to sleep and then awake, I will affirm my passions.

3. I will release my passions to the Universe and Creator. I will trust that the outcome will be as it should be through acceptance.

4. I will live in the present. I will accept things as they are and know that the future will manifest through my Passion and Purpose.

Written Exercises for the Traditions of Mother Earth

Write out your responses to these exercises in this book, on a separate sheet of paper or journal, so you can contemplate your own thoughts and writings for more clarity and meaning.

1. Are you doing things right now to preserve the quality of life that Mother Earth has given to us? What actions are you taking?

2. Are you sacrificing in a sacred way to receive all those things you are worthy of? Do you tend to take the easy way out and not deal with your discomfort?

3. Do you believe that "we are all related"? If so, how and has it had a positive effect on you and those around you?

4. What are your three top passions? How are you pursuing them?

5. How have Passion and Purpose manifested in your life?

6. Are you stuck in the past or future and unable to accept the "Present"?

The Direction of Self and All My Relations ~ Brown ~ Detachment with Love

This sixth direction is the sacred place of Self and All My Relations. Many times, this direction is the most neglected. We know how to take care of ourselves, but often neglect our other relations. Or we pay more attention to others, and neglect ourselves. The universal flow of cosmic energy must flow through all things. This energy flows to balance and harmonize in everything, including us.

When I speak of "All My Relations," I mean all things living, as well as non-living, and not simply our families. As we begin to understand how all things are in relation to one another, we finally realize that we are dependent on all things in the Universe. This is a symbiotic exchange of energy.

Physically, we must get plenty of rest, eat the right things, exercise, and be careful not to put mood-altering chemicals into our bodies to alter our states of consciousness. We must respect our bodies and eat in moderation. America is the most over-fed nation in the world. Hence, it is considered the most obese nation in the world. I try to get plenty of exercise, eat appropriately, and get plenty of rest. I do not drink alcohol or put mood-altering chemicals in my body. A few years ago, I weighed over three hundred pounds, and now I am 100 pounds lighter. I am an elder now, and feel as though I am in my thirties.

How many hours do we spend in front of the television set instead of doing things for ourselves or our families? How can we realize our own passions by spending hours watching others realize theirs? How many hours do you spend watching television? Instead of relaxing with a drink or smoking, I often take a walk, experience nature, meditate, or just be quiet.

These simple activities will relax and calm you naturally without harming your body. As a counselor, I have heard countless excuses for getting high on drugs and alcohol and even made a few myself in my earlier years.

In reality, we tend to rationalize, minimize, and justify our behaviors for using harmful chemicals. We do this because we get into a state of denial. We do not like to think that there are things wrong with us or that we have become addicted to these chemicals. Other addictions to such things as food, work, sex, gambling, TV, and the Internet are all symptoms of a much larger picture. To get to the root of these problems, we must allow ourselves to be treated for these addictions.

Mentally, we must allow our minds to be free of distractions. We must enable the flow of energy to be unrestricted. Energy should flow freely from our minds into the Universe. One of the best ways to quiet our minds of all the clutter of the world is meditation. Guided imagery and relaxation are other ways of renewing our mental health. One advantage of these holistic remedies is that they are free. As a society, we have been programmed to think anything worthwhile costs us money.

As a soldier in Vietnam, I experienced a lot of drug use. We had problems from time to time with the "juicers" and the "heads." The "juicers" were the soldiers who primarily drank alcohol, while the "heads" primarily used drugs. It could be deadly to take someone into combat who was under the influence or detoxifying from their drug of choice, which was usually heroin or speed. These individuals could get you and your men killed. There was a saying in Vietnam, "Free your mind; your ass will follow." What that meant then, as well as now, is when your body, mind, and spirit are free of mood-altering chemicals, you will usually make the right decisions in your life.

Your feelings and emotions play a huge role in dealing with the direction of "All Your Relations." A person I knew allowed herself to get very upset when dealing with a painful divorce and the way her ex-husband treated her children. Specifically, he used the children as weapons against his ex-wife. That action put her children in the middle and hurt them very much. His inability to be a nurturing parent affected her to the point of making her physically ill. She also felt her emotional well-being was contingent on her ability to deal with her children and ex-husband. Consequently, it manifested into her physical self and she became ill. To my knowledge, she did not receive the counseling I recommended, and ultimately and unfortunately died of cancer. I feel that if she had received the help she needed, she might have survived. It's almost as if she just gave up.

There are people who will not only think negative things, but also say negative things about us. For our emotional wellness, we must deflect these negative emotions. If we don't, we will constantly be in turmoil. Another person I know can have a hundred people tell him how great he is and flood him with compliments, but if one person tells him what he perceives as something negative, he will instead focus on the negative, rather than letting it go.

Spiritually, we must allow that sacred flow of spirit to take priority in our lives. Our lives are meaningless if we do not. Without the flow of spirit in our lives, we cannot deal with day-to-day obstacles.

The Direction of Self (remember, you are also one of the "All Your Relations") is associated with the tradition of *Detachment with Love*. Let us talk for a moment about symbols and our attachment to them.

To create whatever you desire, live in the wisdom of uncertainty. Attachment to symbols like money, cars, clothes, or houses does not last. Attachment allows you to feel meaningless, because you exchange yourself for the symbols of self. People who seek to attain security often chase these fleeting symbols throughout their lives.

Attachment to symbols is based on fear and insecurity. Security is never achieved through money alone. Security is only an illusion. The search for security is attachment to the things we know. The things we know are from the conditioning of our past. Because of this, there is no flow of energy.

Uncertainty means stepping into the unknown. It means taking risks. The unknown is always new and fresh, always open to creativity. When you detach with love from the known into the unknown, you step into the realm of all that is possible. Faith is knowing when you step off the edge into the abyss, there will be something there to put your feet upon or you will learn to fly.

A few years ago, I was offered a Program Director's position in Kotzebue, Alaska. I was excited about it because I have always been an adventuresome person. But I was also fearful of the unknown. I took the job and experienced a part of the world few people have ever seen. From my apartment window in Alaska, I could see Kotzebue Sound. On cold mornings I could see seals, whales, and more fish than I could ever imagine. If I had not taken the risk, I would have never experienced that beautiful land.

When you experience uncertainty, relish it. Live in that moment. You will feel alive.

In 1984, after completing my first Sacrifice Lodge, my Ceremonial Grandfather approached me and said he was making me a Ceremonial Grandfather. I was afraid because I thought it was out of my reach after just completing my first lodge. He was adamant in his feelings about my assuming this role to help others. I finally conceded with his approval and have been on this journey for many years now. I had to detach from the known into the unknown to continue on this sacred journey and have helped many in the process.

In the tradition of Detachment with Love, you do not have the need to force solutions. The solutions to problems emerge almost magically out of chaos and uncertainty. Open your mind to the concept that within every problem is a solution and you begin to look at your life in a whole new way. You will learn from every problem in your life. It will have a solution. You will seize opportunities by living in the wisdom of uncertainty. Solutions will appear when your preparation meets opportunity. When you *detach with love*, the solutions to all your problems will come by relinquishing your attachment to the known and journeying into the unknown.

The Tradition of Self

Detachment with Love

Today, I will put the traditions of Self and Detachment with Love in my life by taking the following steps:

1. Today I will cleanse myself in ceremony to rid myself of any impurities I may have picked up unknowingly. I will also meditate once in the morning, and once in the evening. I will ask my ancestors for guidance in my journey. I will transcend my past and ask Creator for forgiveness. I will forgive myself. I will accept where I am today. I will change those things I can. I will ask Creator for the wisdom to know the difference.

2. Today, I will Detach with Love from the symbols of Self. Money, cars, clothes, or houses are fleeting in my life. Security is an illusion. Attachment to symbols is based on fear and insecurity. The search for security is attachment to the things we know. The things we know are conditionings of our past. Because of this, there is no flow of energy.

3. Today, I will Detach with Love from the known and step into the unknown. In doing so, I will step into the realm of all that is possible.

4. Today, I will have the perception that within every problem there is a solution. I will seize the opportunity by living in the wisdom of uncertainty.

Written Exercises for the Tradition
of Self and Detachment

Write out the responses to these exercises in this book, on a separate sheet of paper, or in your journal so you can contemplate your own thoughts and writings for more clarity and meaning.

1. What can you do physically, mentally, emotionally, and spiritually for yourself and all your relations? How are you doing this? If not, what could you do differently?

2. What does *Detachment with Love* mean to you?

3. Have you ever tried to force solutions to your problems instead of letting them emerge out of uncertainty and chaos? What happens when you do this?

4. Are you fearful of uncertainty? If so, what could you do to change this?

Notes

The Direction of the Creator ~ Sky Blue ~ Spirituality

The direction of Creator is the most important of all the directions. Without this direction, all other directions are meaningless.

My relationship with Creator has not always been a positive one. In my early years, Christianity was a major part of my life. I was raised in the Methodist Church and listened to the hellfire-and-brimstone teachings of my church. It was hard for me to visualize, but I could only see God as an avenging, old, white man with a long, flowing beard and long, white hair. I could never fully relate to that God. For one thing he was white, and I was Native American. All I could perceive was an angry, old, white man who waited for me to make mistakes or sin. If I did the latter, at death, he would turn me over to Satan and I would burn in Hell for all eternity.

When I served my country in Vietnam, I experienced things that few people ever dreamed of. I saw the inhumanity and hatred of people. I saw things that, thankfully, most people will never see. Once, when our unit had traveled down Highway One in Vietnam, we stopped at a village where we usually paused to do some bartering with the locals. Just minutes before, the Viet Cong enemy soldiers, had gone through the village and killed several people who were sympathetic to the U.S. soldiers. The Viet Cong had tortured and killed several locals whom I knew.

As I viewed the bodies in disbelief, I saw a young pregnant woman, not dead. Her belly had been split open by the Viet Cong and her baby had been removed from her body. By appearances, the baby had then been thrown against a tree and killed. As I looked at this horrible sight, I was physically sickened. I could not believe that human beings could treat each other in this way.

Witnessing more and more atrocities on both sides during the war, I began to get hardened by what I saw. My mind, to protect my sanity, began to look at such horrific acts and the bodies as just objects with no sacredness or life attached to them. I began to question God, as I knew him. I thought if there was a God, why would he allow things like this to happen. I began to view the whole world as an unholy place.

When I returned from Vietnam, I was inducted into four Warrior Societies and given a hero's welcome. Inside, however, I was a broken man who had been traumatized by the war. I began to drink more and more to quiet the demons and ghosts haunting me. The drinking and drugs only sedated me for a while until I woke up. I really began to wonder about my sanity and often thought about suicide. On four different occasions, I put a weapon to my head or in my mouth, trying to get the nerve to end it all.

I was discharged from the military in 1973 at Fort Sill, Oklahoma. Ten years later, I was drinking myself to death, as were so many of my fellow warriors. In August 1983, 1 was admitted to the Clinton Regional Hospital in Clinton, Oklahoma and was dying. At the time, I could have cared less if I lived or died. After all, I felt that God had deserted me. I felt like no one cared, especially God. I felt that God would never forgive me for taking lives, even in war.

My mother was the only one who came to see me while I was in the hospital. All others had given up on me. I could not blame them because I had already given up on myself. She pleaded with me to stop this insanity. She asked me to go to Wyoming to talk with my elders, who were involved in our ceremonial ways. Even during my self-destructive days, I never stopped loving my mother and I respected her.

With love, I agreed to go to Wyoming as soon as I could travel. Once in Wyoming, I was met by my uncle, Adam Shakespeare. I explained my intent to him and he took me to see the Intercessor of our Sacred Lodge. I gave this man an offering, explained my intent, and made a vow to go into the Sacrifice Lodge. I attribute this act to my recovery and thereby saved my life. I have not had to make the excuse for using any mind-altering chemicals to influence my state of consciousness since the summer of 1983.

Creator had never turned His back on me; I turned my back on Him. He carried me through Vietnam, through the fits of anger and violence, the deaths of family and friends, the suicide attempts. Most importantly, He gave me the strength and courage to finish the lodges I had vowed to complete.

I cannot speak of what exactly goes on during this ceremony except to say that it is extremely difficult and that the person undergoes severe challenges throughout this ordeal.

Despite all the times I turned my back on Creator, he continued to love me. He never gave up on me. He never gave me more than He and I could handle in a single day. Today, Creator is my friend. I talk to Him every day. He has forgiven me my transgressions. He loves me unconditionally.

The Creator direction is associated with spirituality. You could say this direction also represents your Spiritual Destiny. There are three traditions associated with this direction. They are Spiritual Self, Talent, and Serving Mankind.

Spiritual Self: We had a saying back in the 1960s and 1970s, to "go out and find yourself." Creator has put us in this human form as spiritual beings to discover our purpose in this lifetime. For us to express this sacred being, we must "find ourselves." I did this through the Spiritual Ceremonies of my People. I needed to challenge myself and sacrifice myself mentally, emotionally, physically, and spiritually. Only then was I able to transcend onto a new path.

Talent: Each and every one of us has unique talents. In some cases, we have many. When we discover these unique talents, they become passions. When you are passionate about something you do, you lose yourself in time because it has purpose and meaning to you. Follow your talents; they were gifted to you by the Creator.

Serving Mankind: When you have unique talents, learn how to best utilize them for the good of mankind. When these factors are combined in a sacred way, you will experience abundance. If you ask, "What can I do?" instead of "What do I get out of this?" your spirit will combine with Creator to produce whatever you want. You will go beyond the ego into the universal spirit.

If you intend to find your destiny, you have to first make commitments to your spirit. The first commitment is: "I will seek my higher spirit through spiritual practice." The second commitment is: "I will enjoy myself through my unique talents and share them with others. In this way, I will experience serenity tranquility, and peace." The third commitment is: "I will serve humanity by sharing my unique talents."

That is how my life unfolded in front of me. Some of it was intentional and some was not. I thought it was the way I had planned it out for myself, but now I realize that it was Creator's plan for me. Everything that happened in my life was for a reason. All things are in Creator's unique plan for all of us. Many times, I did not know why my life was unfolding as it was but it was all for a reason. Everything that has happened in my life has prepared me for this moment. Most things I have learned from. Others things, I am still learning.

It's almost like a dance—the dance of life. We keep dancing until we get most of the moves just right. Some moves we will never master, but we keep trying. I still manage to step on the toes of my dancing partners, but most forgive me. So you know what? I think I'll just keep on dancing until I get it right.

This concludes our reading of the seventh direction. As you complete your reading for today, I ask you to consider the activities on the following pages.

The Direction of Creator

The Tradition of Destiny

Today, I will put the direction of Creator and the tradition of Destiny in my life by taking the following steps:

1. Today, I will cleanse myself in ceremony to rid myself of any impurities I may have picked up unknowingly. I will also meditate, once in the morning and once in the evening. I will ask my ancestors for guidance in my journey. I will transcend my past and ask Creator for forgiveness. I will forgive myself. I will accept where I am today. I will change those things I can. I will ask Creator for wisdom to know the difference.

2. Today, I will look deep into my soul to find my true spiritual self. I will awaken this spirit to the true sacredness of the universe and all my relations.

3. Today, I will serve humanity by making a list of my talents and using them for all. In doing so, I will experience serenity, tranquility, and peace. This will create affluent abundance in my life.

4. I will ask myself daily, "How can I best serve mankind." The answer will flow with love to humanity.

Written Exercises for the

Traditions of Creator

Write out your responses to these exercises in this book, on a separate sheet of paper, or in your journal so you can contemplate your own thoughts and writings for more clarity and meaning.

1. How does Creator fit into your life at this time?
   How does that feel to you?

2. Was there ever a time you turned your back on Creator?
   What was the outcome?

3. What do you think your destiny is? Do you feel passionate about it?

4. What is the most important talent you have right now? How can you best serve humanity with this talent?

The Dream

This is a story of a vision I had while sleeping during the Arapaho Sundance in Ethete, Wyoming, in July, 2004. I had been under great stress after my car broke down in Colorado and I had to borrow money from friends to get three of my daughters to Wyoming for the ceremonies.

I was feeling the great burden of how I was going to overcome all the obstacles I had ahead of me. I was burdened not only by the financial burden of the trip from Oklahoma to Wyoming, and back, but now the responsibility of three young daughters. As a single father, my former wife often allowed me to bring our daughters to ceremonies, as we both felt it was important for the girls to learn about their People.

As I lay in my sleeping bag in my teepee that night, I wondered how I would get through this tremendous problem. I remember how helpless and hopeless I felt, to the point of tears. I dozed in and out of sleep and was taken back to the time I was baptized at the age of twelve at the Angie Smith Memorial Church in Oklahoma City, Oklahoma.

My mother was very ill and hospitalized at this time and I was so worried about her. I decided on my own to get baptized, hoping that Creator would come into my life and bless my mother with recovery. For the first time in my young life, I felt the existence of something more powerful than anything I had ever experienced. This new relationship felt so wonderful. It was short-lived.

I drifted in and out of the church until the age of thirteen, when I started drinking alcohol. The alcohol slowly took the sacredness of Creator from my life. My life felt meaningless with alcohol. I began to get into trouble because of my drinking. I graduated from high school in 1967 and continued to drink.

I tried college for a while but flunked out by keeping late hours and continuing to drink. I got married and had my first child, but was still drinking. I became abusive to my first wife. She left me and I was about to get into serious trouble because of child support. Our attorneys thought the best thing for my wife and child was for me to enlist in the military so I could provide a Class Q allotment for them.

Not wanting to be incarcerated, I joined the U. S. Army in March of 1970. After several months of basic training at Fort Lewis, Washington, and then advanced training in Fort Eustice, Virginia, I shipped out for Vietnam in October of 1970. If there any remnants of Christianity and spirituality existed in my life, I lost them there.

I was a young Christian man thrust into war by society and experienced so many unholy acts against humanity. Upon returning to the States from my tour of duty in Vietnam, I was diagnosed with Post-Traumatic Stress Disorder, PTSD. My drinking and drug problem became worse. I continued to drink and do drugs for many years after I got out of the service in 1973. I was in and out of drug and alcohol treatment centers with no luck. Friends and family literally gave up on me. I drank and ingested drugs so much that by 1983, I was dying. I was hemorrhaging so badly that the doctors were barely able to save my life.

Through much hard work at my sobriety, and my belief in Christ, I have been clean and sober since August 8, 1983. I tell you this for it is important to understand that while I am a Ceremonial Man for my People, I still consider myself to be a Christian.

As I lay there in my teepee that night trying to figure out a solution to the obstacles in front of me, I again began to question my faith. It was almost too much to bear. I asked Jesus Christ, his father Creator, and the "Old Man" to listen to my prayer. The "Old Man" is the Arapaho Sacred Flat Pipe used as a conduit to Creator for prayer.

I had difficulty sleeping that night, but finally drifted off in prayer and began to dream. I saw myself in a village of some kind, somewhat like the villages I remembered from Vietnam. There were gardens everywhere and everything was very beautiful. I went to the porch of one of the huts and sat down in a chair. I began to see people running in fear. I became alarmed when many men and women came to me asking for help. One woman cried out, "You must help us! You are the only one who can help."

I said, "What can I do? I don't know how to help you."

All of a sudden, I noticed an old Indian man standing on the porch. He was dressed in traditional Native attire. He had on buckskins and four eagle feathers were tied in his long white hair. His moccasins were beaded in old traditional Arapaho designs. He said, "The enemy is coming closer. You must help your people."

I said, "I am only one man, what can I do?"

The Old Man said, "There is a basement downstairs and many men have struggled to open the door to it, but they cannot. You are the only one who can open it. In it, you will find everything you need to conquer the enemy. This will be the first of four miracles I will show you for you to believe."

He looked at me and said, "You don't believe, do you?"

I looked at him and said, "No!"

The Old Man looked at me and quietly said, "All you have to do is have faith and trust in Creator."

I stood there before the door. It was a huge sliding stone door. I thought, "All these other men have tried to move the door and to no avail. What good could I do?"

The Old Man again said, "Have faith and trust in Creator."

I stood in front of the door and with all my strength, I began to move the door. The gap grew wider and wider, until the door had completely slid open. As I gazed into the room of the basement, I expected to see weapons of all kinds. Instead I saw Ceremonial pipes, traditional medicines, and many things sacred to me.

I looked at the Old Man and he just smiled. I didn't know what to think. How could we win without conventional weapons? I looked at him again and asked, "What are the other miracles you promised to show me?"

The Old Man said, "Look up there." And he pointed to the moon, so big and bright.

I looked at the moon and soon saw something coming from behind it. I saw just a flicker at first. The flicker soon became larger and larger. As it got closer, I gaped in disbelief when I saw an angel before me. As it hovered in front of me, I noticed the angel was someone who had recently passed. The angel looked at me and smiled with much love in its heart.

In my dream, I began to feel very emotional and began to weep. I looked at the Old Man and asked him, "It's true, isn't it? When we die, we go to a much better place?"

He repeated, "Have faith and trust in Creator." I felt I was in the presence of something much greater than all of mankind.

Still not quite believing what I was witnessing, I said to the Old Man, "All right, I have opened the door for the first miracle and witnessed the angel, but that was only two miracles."

He said, "Look up again." I looked up again and from behind the moon, I witnessed thousands of angels coming down to earth. As they got closer and closer, I began to see many friends, family, and so many ancestors.

I began to cry more and more, not believing what I was witnessing. I was so overcome with emotion that I felt that I might faint. I looked at the Old Man, who just smiled.

I asked, "Why am I witnessing these things?"

He said, "Because you don't believe. All Creator wants for you is to have faith and trust in Him. That's all He has ever wanted. So many like you go through life never being able to realize that there are so many miracles before them. He just wants you to know how much He loves you and all of His children."

Again, somewhat still disbelieving what I had just witnessed, I asked, "You promised me four miracles. That was just three.

Old Man again looked at me disappointedly and said, "You still don't quite believe, do you?"

I had to admit, I was still skeptical. A big grin began to move across his face and he said, "Have faith and trust in Creator." And he added, "You don't know, do you?"

Puzzled, I replied, "Know what?"

"You are the fourth miracle," the Old Man said.

"Me?" I asked, startled.

He just nodded. "In Creator's love for you, He has let you see the miracles of life. Even when you didn't believe, He still loved you just the way He has all through your life when you have forsaken him. He loves you that much."

I felt very small when the Old Man said these words to me. He was right, of course. Creator has never left me. All I have to do is ask for His help.

The Old Man said, "All you need to help the People is what Creator has given you in ceremony and nothing else. You cannot fight against these odds with mere guns and ammunition. You have to fight with love, peace, and compassion. This is the only way to win. You have to use the medicine He has given you."

My heart filled with so much serenity, tranquility, and peace. I began to weep, somewhat out of guilt but mostly out of joy.

I awoke from my dream and felt wetness on my face. I had actually been crying in my sleep. As I wiped the tears from my face, I looked up at the opening by the flaps of the teepee, and saw a small white light going up towards the opening and then going out in the heavens.

It did not frighten me because my uncle Adam Shakespeare, who had given me the spirit of "Scotty" to protect me years before, had said, "When you see this light or a small feather floating, don't be frightened, it's only 'Scotty' protecting you and people praying for you in a good way."

As I continued to look at the stars in the night sky, I felt the presence of Creator all around me. My heart was so full of love for Creator.

Afterword

The Seven Sacred Directions and Traditions are best expressed in all of creation. Everything that is, was, or shall be is the result of conscious choice-making. Down to the basic cell level of all things, every situation that occurs is because of appropriate responses to those circumstances. That is the *Tradition of the Circle*.

Every living cell reacts because of the constant flow of energy to that cell. It is the constant give and take of the Universe. Every minute molecule and atom reacts in a symbiotic dance of life to support one another. That is the universal *Tradition of the Giveaway*.

The *Tradition of Spirit* is activated through silence, communion with Mother Earth, being non-judgmental, and being quiet in your spirit. In this state of calm, you can begin to introduce any intent that you may wish. If your intent is sincere, it will come to pass.

There are three basic components to the **Tradition of No Resistance**. The first is **Acceptance**. Everything Creator has given you in this point in time is as it should be. When you can accept people, places, and things in this very moment, you are experiencing unconditional love to all of creation.

The second component of this tradition is **Responsibility**. Simply stated, this means not blaming anyone, anything, or yourself for your situation in the moment. As you slowly begin to realize this, every person, place, or thing will become your teacher.

The third component of this tradition is **Defenselessness**. This means that you no longer have the need to convince or persuade others of your point of view. You will prevent an argument if you have no point to defend.

When you begin to introduce your intent or purpose, you activate possibilities beyond your comprehension. Your focused purpose initiates the universal flow of energy to fulfill your purpose and passion. If your purpose does not violate any sacred laws of the Universe, you can have or be whatever your heart desires. This is the **Tradition of Passion and Purpose**.

To create whatever you desire, you have to live in the wisdom of uncertainty. Attachment to symbols like money, cars, clothes, or houses is a transient thing. This act allows you to feel meaningless because you exchange yourself for symbols. Uncertainty is stepping into the unknown. It means taking risks. This is the **Tradition of Detachment with Love**. When you detach with love from the known into the unknown, you step into the realm of all that is possible.

There are three characteristics associated with the **Tradition of Spiritual Destiny**. The first is the **Spiritual Self**. Creator put us in human form as spiritual beings to find out what our purpose in this life is. In order for us to express this sacred being, we must "find ourselves." The second is **Talent**. Each and every one of us has unique talents. In some cases, we have many. When we discover what these unique talents are, they become passions. When you are passionate about something you do, you lose yourself in time because it has purpose and meaning to you. The third is **Serving Mankind**. When you understand how to serve mankind with your unique talents, you destiny is right in front of you.

When these factors are combined in a sacred way, you will experience abundance.

If you read this book a chapter a day for the next week and then reread for four weeks total, you will attain an understanding of the traditions and directions through processing and examining your own life. When you see in your own words and review what you have written in the exercises, you will gain clarity and insight into your life as Creator would have it.

There is no quick fix for situations in our lives, but if you are sincere in your efforts to experience the Seven Sacred Directions and apply them to your life, you will know serenity, tranquility, and peace, and create whatever your heart desires. You will experience joy like you have never known before.

Native American Wedding Ceremony

Singing Man, Southern Arapaho, April 27, 2004

EAST ~ RED

My love for you is like the East direction,
From where the morning star rises,
From where everything begins anew like the spring,
Where we are beginning our lives.
Blessings to the sacred direction of the East,
I will honor you with my love, always.

SOUTH~YELLOW

My love for you is like the South direction, Summer
Where everything is in full bloom,
Full of life where the sun is at its highest,
Our love will bloom like the flowers of summer.
Blessings to the sacred direction of the South,
I will honor you with my love, always.

WEST ~ BLACK

My love for you is like the West direction
Where everything is full of mystery,
Where Mother Earth is starting to get sleepy.
Our love will be guided by our ancestors, who dwell in this place,
Like our ancestors, we will be quiet and still;
We will listen to our hearts and our love for each other.
Blessings to the sacred direction of the West
I will honor you with my love, always.

NORTH ~ WHITE

My love for you is like the North direction
Where everything sleeps beneath the white cover of winter.
My love for you will never die.
My love will be in the care of the wisdom keepers of the North,
Like the wisdom of the elders.
Our love will continue to grow until our hair is white like the snow.
Blessings to the sacred direction of the North
I will honor you with my love, always.

MOTHER EARTH ~ GREEN

My love for you is like the Mother Earth direction
Where everything is nurtured by Mother Earth,
Our love for each other will be nurtured with each passing season,
Like Mother Earth, as long as we take care of her,
She will take care of us,
I will take care of you always.
I will be strong like Mother Earth,
Our love will last as long as the rivers flow and the grass grows.
Blessings to the sacred direction of Mother Earth,
I will honor you with my love, always.

MYSELF ~ BROWN

My love for you is like the direction of Self and All My Relations
Where I will continue to honor myself as Creator wishes,
As long as we take care of our individual selves and all our relations,
We honor Creator for giving us life.
This day is Creator's gift to us.
What we do with it is our gift to Creator.
By honoring myself and my relations, I will honor you.
Blessings to the sacred direction of Self,
I will honor you with my love, always.

CREATOR ~ SKY BLUE

My love for you is like the direction of Creator,
where all things are sacred and holy.
Creator has blessed me with you, and I to you,
as we begin this sacred and holy journey.
I will honor Creator by honoring you as my wife and I as your husband
Thank you, Creator for this wonderful blessing,
and the blessing of our unborn children.
Blessings to the sacred direction of Creator,
I will honor you with my love, always.

About the Author

E-NAN-NEE-BAY-EE, Singing Man, was born at the Clinton Indian Hospital in Clinton, Oklahoma. He is descended from a long line of Chiefs and Warriors from both sides of his family. His mother, Killing After, is full-blooded Southern Arapaho. His father, White Eagle, was half Pawnee and half Kiowa. He is very proud to belong to four warrior societies. The Kiowa *Ton-Kon-Ga* (Black Leggings), who fought the U.S. Cavalry and *Federales* by lashing their bodies to the ground to signify "fighting to the death," the Kiowa-Apache Blackfeet Society, and the Star Hawk Society. Singing Man is also the Executive Officer of the Oklahoma Intertribal Vietnam Veteran's Honor/Color Guard.

Singing Man served in the U. S. Army from 1970 to 1973, becoming a veteran of the Vietnam War in 1970-71. He was decorated twelve times while serving.

In 1983, he started his spiritual journey and began to follow the "Red Road" through the spiritual ceremonies of his people. He is also a state and internationally certified counselor who has been assisting others for thirty years in the mental health field. Singing Man is now retired and assists those who ask for help. Please visit the website, www.sevensacreddirections.weebly.com/singingman.html, for more information.

MavenMark Books is a division of HenschelHAUS Publishing, Inc.
We are happy to review manuscripts from new and veteran authors
and offer a wide range of author services,
such as coaching, editing, design, and book marketing.

Please visit www.HenschelHAUSBooks.com for submission guidelines,
our on-line bookstore, and calendar of workshops and author events.